Let's Write A Story

SEVEN WAYS TO PLOT

Sue Viders and Becky Martinez

DENVER, CO

Let's Write A Story/ Sue Viders and Becky Martinez—1st ed.
ISBN 978-0-942011-17-3

Contents

Before You Start   1

Basics of Plot   4

Developing Your Plot   11

Three Acts   17

Outline   26

Plot Points   31

Storyboards   39

Backward Plotting   46

No Plotting   50

Examples   56

Introduction

If you are one of those people who have been saying that you want to write a novel, but you have no idea how to go about it, this book is aimed at helping you. We're here to help you get started. By the time you finish reading this book, you should have a good idea about how to construct a plot for your story or at least a general idea about how to get started on creating a plot from beginning to end.

We have worked for years writing fiction and non-fiction books, articles and stories. We've also spent many long hours researching writing techniques and then used that information to help beginning and intermediate writers. Twelve years ago we began critiquing together and realized we shared many common goals in our efforts to help other writers. Since then we have worked with many would-be or aspiring writers on creating plots, developing characters, and helping those writers get their stories into order through a wide variety of workshops, in-person presentations, and online classes. We have taught classes on everything from how to develop characters, character personalities, character arcs, building villains to different ways to plot. We even spent time constructing a plotting method of our own and it will be offered in an upcoming book.

Helping others has helped our own writing process too, and we've learned a great deal as we coached and taught dozens of writers how to get their stories started, how to bring their characters to life on the page and how to get from a simple idea to a fully fleshed-out plot. As a result we have now have taken the material we collected over the years through research and classes and put it all together into a series of simple, easy to follow booklets. They are aimed at helping writers on all levels – from those starting out in the writing process to those who have already written books and who might be looking for different techniques to try.

One thing we have learned through all our years of teaching and writing our own books – no two writers plot or write the exact same way. Sue is a careful plotter, while Becky prefers to let the ideas percolate and write with her muse on her shoulder. This book and our future booklets have been written with that in mind. No matter how you choose to plot – whether you want to come up with a detailed outline or if you prefer to start out with just a skeleton sketch, or fly by the seat of your pants with no more than a simple idea, this book can help you begin to get your plotting ideas in order and start writing your own work of fiction.

On the following pages are several different ways/methods/systems of plotting. But understand there is no one perfect way. What you might consider doing is to try creating your story with different plotting methods that appeal to you. Then decide which works best for you. Sue uses a combination creating a strong main character, then the timeline outline, the scene by scene and the storyboard. Becky comes up with a plot idea, a list of characters, an ending and then begins to create scenes until she arrives at the end.

Also note that some methods seem to work best with different genres. For example, when writing a detailed mystery or thriller, doing an outline along with a timeline is almost essential in order to keep the sequence of events in order. Some mystery writers also make a timeline for their villain so they know what the antagonist is up to throughout the story.

For an adventure or quest story, Christopher Vogler's *Hero's Journey* method works extremely well. If you are writing fantasy or science fiction, you might look into Vogler's method as well as the works of Joseph Campbell, a well-known mythologist, who has also published books on writing mythology. If you are writing romance, the storyboard can help greatly in planning the major turning points in a love affair. Because most romance publishers want the story told in both the hero and heroine's Points of View (POV), a storyboard can also be useful to keep track of how much time each character is getting in the book and where changes in POV take place.

You don't have to do everything in every method, but you will find that even a bit of planning BEFORE you start writing will really help with the overall story. You will have a better sense of direction and more clearly understand what needs to happen to make the final outcome satisfying to the reader. We also recommend completing a character arc as you plot, especially one with the emotional or internal factors/reactions woven into the action scenes.

Some writers like to plot on the computer, while others simply do it in their head. Many will work on paper, and there are some who use 3x5 index cards or sticky notes so they can move the plot and the characters around easily. Others might use computer programs, such as Scrivener or the Snowflake method to help with plotting. Some writers will jot down notes on scraps of paper and then put them into order. Some even use the "Notes" or "Memo" function on their cell phones to work out their plot. These days, a plot idea can be detailed any time and any place.

If you are one of those writers who prefer to come up with detailed character outlines first, then we recommend you go in that direction. Get to know those characters, their conflicts and then work out their motives and reactions. Write out your character profiles. Some writers spend long hours doing this. In the end you can still come out with a plot that works as long as you don't spend all your time on the character sketches and little time on the plot. Once you have developed those characters, put them into action through your plot.

Because there are so many different methods, and since each writer needs to personally discover and determine the method that works best for them, we strongly suggest you study each of the various methods and systems that follow. Each one has something great to offer. You may even find that a combination of several methods works best for you.

Good luck!

SUE & BECKY

CHAPTER 1

Before You Start

No matter how you choose to plot, no story is ever going to jump off the drawing board into a book fully plotted. A book's plot will have too many variables for that. Even the best authors can't go straight from idea to finished product in just a few days. In most cases the plot will be the product of days or even weeks of work. Once you begin to write, you may still discover that the plot is going nowhere or the characters are meandering or refusing to do what you as the author want them to do. That is where knowing the plotting process or coming up with various ideas for a plot can help you.

One constant in plotting is that every story starts with an idea. It can be an idea about a story, a location or a character. It can be a sentence-long thought, a fleeting whisper of a generality or it can be a fully developed profile. You might want to write a book based on a character you've known or tell a loose interpretation of a story you've heard. You might want your story to focus on an event or on a different world or want it to drive home a universal truth to your readers. Your idea might be futuristic or lodged in the past or in a fictional realm or a real city. You might even want to invent some new types of beings or use real people from history.

Everything begins with your idea—whatever it might be. No matter where you get the idea or what it is, what is important is to know you should have an idea of some sort to start your book. Remember, as the author, you can always change it later.

Once you have your idea, then you must begin to develop a character. It can be one, it can be many, but you will need people in your book. To keep things simple, start out with one or two characters and work with them. Again, you can always begin to develop others later, but if you don't have a main character or several main characters, you won't have a story.

Even if you are writing about the overthrow of the planet, an infamous murder or a simple love story, you will want to tell the story through the eyes of a person or several people. Choose your main characters and then give them a PROBLEM.

They will **need** to have something they **need** to do, whether it's find love, overcome a threat, solve a crime, or save the world.

A plot should revolve around a character with a problem that needs to be solved.

Next, make that problem personal to your character or characters. Readers will love stories where people have problems, whether it is two teenagers falling in love, a woman trying to save the planet or a family fighting Zombies.

One way you as the author can make that problem more personal to you is by naming your characters as early as possible. A character with a name comes alive more completely than this strange being floating out in space. You don't need to name them all, but at least give your main character or characters a first name before you begin.

CHAPTER 2

Basics of a Plot

Plotting your book is critical because without a cohesive plot, your book is going nowhere. The plot is like a skeleton. It holds the body together. Without it, you're going to have a lot of skin and tissue or plenty of substance but it will be without any sort of form. The plot is what forms the backbone and the skeletal extensions for your book. You can start at the head and go all the way down to the toes or at the toes or fingertips, but by the time you're finished you need to have that firm, skeletal structure in place.

Now, having said all that, there are so many different ways to plot that a writer could end up with a spinning head when he/she sets out to create the plot and starts getting the story down on paper or into the computer.

As we've noted, some writers rely on detailed outlines or copious pages of notes. One well-known writer described his outline as his first draft. Others say that if they take the time to write an outline they feel that the book is written and they don't want to go back and finish the book. Still others just sit down and simply write without any sort of preparation, other than their initial idea. In this booklet, we are going to let you choose your own plotting method and figure out what might work best for you. We will give you a series of different ways to plot and you can experiment with each method and learn what makes the most sense to you. Are you detail oriented or would you rather leave things to chance? Do you need to know the exact beginning and ending? Would you rather let the characters determine the course of your book? The choice is yours.

No matter which method works best for you, you will learn there are certain things you need to know to guide you as you start to write your book. Everyone who writes a novel for the commercial fiction marketplace has to answer these five questions before starting, no matter what plotting formula that writer uses.

WHO is the main character?
WHAT is the story about?
WHEN is it happening?
WHERE is it happening?
WHY is it happening?

These elements are all necessary for any story, and starting with them at the very beginning can help you to get just about any simple idea off the ground and headed in the direction of a complete novel.

WHO is the Main Character?

First of all, and perhaps most importantly, let's go back to that character we mentioned earlier. You need to think of your characters every step along the way as you plot your book. A fast-moving plot without a compelling character is going nowhere. The reader needs to have some investment in the story and that comes from developing a character the reader wants to know, someone with whom the reader can share adventures and trials and tribulations. Think of the books you love best. Was it the story that drew you, or the characters? Or both?

The *Wizard of Oz* was a fun adventure, an interesting tale in its own right, but it was more than just an amusing fantasy story. We came to like Dorothy and to cheer for her as she faced adversity. We wanted her to defeat the Wicked Witch and get back home to Kansas. We enjoyed her new friends.

The same is true of Scarlett O'Hara. She was vain and selfish in *Gone with the Wind,* but would we have wanted to watch her story unfold before the Civil War? She would have been just another spoiled Southern Belle. Telling the story against the backdrop of the Civil War gave us a heroine we suffered with, cheered for and cried with as she tried to win the man of her dreams—the wrong man. We knew long before she did that Rhett Butler was the right man even as he alternately pursued her and walked away from her.

Your character and your story need to work hand in hand to weave an interesting and compelling tale. Your main character may be a hero at the beginning, but be certain to then give him or her a story worthy of his/her status, something they find themselves unable to conquer or you can exploit their weaknesses and nearly bring them to their knees before they triumph. Even Superman has Kryptonite as his weakness, so the author gives it to the bad guys to battle him and nearly bring about his downfall.

Your character needs to have a plot worthy of his/her efforts and the plot also needs to be geared toward that particular character.

Keep in mind, when we mention characters, this can be anyone from the hero to the heroine, to the villain, to an outer space monster. This is the character that the story is about, the character who is the focus of the story. This is the person around whom you need to build your plot. A plot where a secondary character becomes more important risks the reader losing interest in your main character. Hannibal Lector is a good example of a minor character taking over a story. He first appeared as a minor character in Thomas Harris' novels *Red Dragon* and *Silence of the Lambs*, but became so important Harris ended up writing two other novels just about his exploits.

You might have two equal characters in a romance with both a hero and heroine getting equal time or you might have a list of characters in an epic fantasy tale, but as you begin you will want to list them and give as much information as you can on each person or entity in your book.

WHAT is happening?

This is here your idea comes into play. Remember we said to give your main character a a problem? This is that problem, the event that changes the main character's life. Is she trying to solve a murder? Do you want him to fall in love with the woman next door? Is he a police detective assigned a murder case? What is the issue at hand? Has the family's life been invaded by aliens? Does she want to help her father get re-installed on the throne? Is he a young wizard going off to wizard boarding school?

This premise can be as large as you want to make it or as small as the one sentence we just listed. From there you can begin to build your plot

WHERE is it happening?

This element of your story is self-explanatory. This is the location for your plot. The story can take place in a city, the country, on the ocean or on another planet. Setting is important because it can play a role in the plot, either by expanding what can happen or limiting it.

Would *Star Wars* have worked if it hadn't been set in a faraway galaxy and involved interplanetary travel? Part of the allure was visiting many different alien worlds and seeing the various creatures and the different beings inhabiting them. Could it have worked if it was set on earth? Yes, but it would have required some changes. Consider the mythic adventure tale of *Jason and the Argonauts.* Jason and his crew were also visiting many unknown places and coming across unknown entities but it took a mythical tale to get in all the strange creatures.

WHEN is it happening?

Just like the location, the "when" or time period can play a major role in how your plot takes place. Is it a futuristic tale or is it set in the old West or in the days or King Arthur? The customs of those time periods will play a role in the plot just as the location does.

If your story is set in the past, research will be needed because the historical facts need to be accurate. Readers who might be interested in a certain time frame probably are very aware of the conventions of the past as well as what might be possible. If you are writing a Steampunk or alternate universe story, you will be allowed to bring items from the future into play or if you are writing a science fiction story then you might be allowed modern technology. Think of the great novels of H. G. Wells or Jules Verne who were writing ahead of their time.

Also be careful with your dialogue. Remember modern slang wasn't used in the Middle Ages and some of today's slang was not used even twenty years ago. Be careful or you might pull the reader totally out of the story.

If the story is set in the present, you can simply draw on your own life's experiences, but again, you will want to be honest and accurate in your setting. Know your location and the distances between places. Google maps can be a good reference if you are uncertain. The satellite view can even show you terrain.

If your story is set in the future, you get to make up everything and let your imagination go wild. Make up words or weapons, but remember as you create your world that if you set certain guidelines, rules or structures you can't simply change them to fit the plot. Your world must stay true to itself, even if it is your creation.

WHY is this event happening?

The **WHY** of any story goes to the MOTIVATION of the main characters. It is the reason the characters act or have to respond. Why is s/he doing this? What is the reason?

They are motivated because their lover, mate has been murdered and they think the police will never find the killer, or are taking too long to find the killer.

They are motivated by guilt or by revenge to overthrow the evil lord/politician who destroyed their father/family.

They are motivated by a need to prove something – either to themselves or to someone else.

They are motivated by circumstances or by being placed in a situation where they need to struggle to survive.

They are motivated by love – perhaps of their family or another person to save the family home or protect their loved ones.

Another way to look at the **WHAT** and **WHY** is...

The WHAT is the *external action* in the story,

while the WHY is the *internal motivation* that causes the character to start his or her journey.

Once you have established all these elements you are ready to progress to the **HOW**.

That will become your plot. **HOW** do the events unfold? The answer is simple. No genre story begins without something that will happen that will set all the following events in motion. Once you have your idea in mind, and you have the principles of your 5 W's, you are ready to start plotting your novel.

CHAPTER 3

Developing Your Plot

Once you have the 5 W's completed you are ready to start putting your idea into a plotting structure. But where do you start? We want to introduce you to a simple way to start your plotting that we have developed through all of our teaching and years of work with thousands of writers. It's a useful method that many of our students and writers have found easy to understand, follow and use.

We call it the **PLOTTING WHEEL**

Think of an old-fashion wagon wheel with twelve spokes radiating from a central hub. Each spoke is a necessary part to hold the wheel and the story together.

Character

The hub is the **Character** or the main person in the plot. The reason Character is in the hub is that the Character MUST interact with all of the various factors/elements for the story to be complete.

Here are the twelve spokes or elements that the character has to interact with:

Circumstances

Every story needs a setting in both place and time so the reader can orient themselves before the actual plot begins. The social milieu or cultural environment also needs to be set up for the character.

Catastrophe

This is what sets the story in motion. The character is faced with a terrible dilemma or a serious problem that needs to be immediately solved or fixed.

Crusade

As a result of the Catastrophe, the character must act and this is what the character/characters set out to do to solve the problem. This is an external goal the character sets or a physical action the character takes.

Cause

This is the "why" or the internal emotional reason the character starts to pursue the external action. The **Crusade** and the **Cause** are two different sides of a coin. You need both of them in order for the character to move forward in the story. Another way to think of them is that they are the physical action and mental reaction to the catastrophe.

Complications

Your character will run into a series of complications or problems as s/he trudges along the road to find the answer/solution to the crusade. These complications, whether external or internal, will keep him/her from getting/finding/or solving the problem

Companions

Your character will not be alone in any novel. He/she will most likely need some help   along the way--friends, family, lover and there will also be a nasty villain.

Clashes

When faced with a Complication, whether physical or emotional, the reaction may create some sort of a Clash. Just like the Complication, these can be external or internal. They might be a physical battle or an internal struggle/decision faced by the hero and heroine. The hero or heroine may not be successful in all of these struggles, but the various Complications and Clashes are good ways to increase action and to fully illustrate and develop your characters. Complications and Clashes can show the emotional strength and/or physical attributes of your characters. These elements also help your characters learn and grow.

Crisis

The Complications and Clashes should continue to increase in intensity throughout the story until all looks lost for your main characters. The crisis is specific event that has to be faced by the main character and his/her companions. But the focus should remain on the main character.   S/he must answer or be part of the final solution. The Crisis is the catalyst for the growing maturity that will lead to the final change.

Change

Now the character has to realize that if s/he doesn't do something different, all will be lost. With this realization comes the final growth and change in the character. In a romance, this is where the main characters realize their love for each other and the strength it gives them personally. It is where they know they can overcome anything through their love.

Climax

This is the final struggle in the story where the bad guy gets his or when one character realizes s/he has to reverse course. This may or may not be related to the beginning goal or the initial reason the character starts on the journey. The character's goals may change along the way depending on the various complications and crises the character will face.

Conclusion

The battle is over. The main character has won the day and all returns to normal and all the loose ends are neatly tied up for the reader. If you are writing a romance, the hero and heroine have confessed their love for each other and overcome any obstacles that might have prevented them from being together.

In some cases the author puts in an epilogue or a final scene. This is often used in the romance/relationship stories where the reader really wants to know what is going to happen to the characters after the final "I love you" is said. It may also be used in a series science fiction, fantasy or mystery as a way to set up the next story in the series. It can be a time right after the resolution scene or months later.

If you go through and fill in quick sketches of all these items using the Plotting Wheel for your story idea, you will find that you are now ready to plot. Let's move on with the process and begin the practical development for YOUR book.

No matter what method you use to plot you must start with the catastrophe, which is often called...

the INCITING INCIDENT

This changes the regular life and world of your main characters. Let's look at some examples from various genres.

Romance – A woman arrives in town looking to make a new life for herself and her young son and meets the man she will eventually love. He is trying to take care of his troubled teenage daughter. Neither is seeking romance, but their meeting will change everything for both.

Mystery – A body is discovered in the river. From this event the police officer might be called upon to investigate, the private detective might be hired by a woman who is suspected of the crime or the relative of the deceased may set out to prove who committed the crime.

Science Fiction – A strange space ship lands in a cornfield and only a farm family sees it and knows it is there. Are the aliens who resemble humans good or are they out to conquer the world?

Fantasy – The young witch casts a spell that whisks her away to a foreign world where she seeks to find her brother who was banished there earlier and she faces unknown wizards and creatures to rescue him.

Once you have set the event that will change a character's life you can begin to build your plot. Let's look at the various methods you might use to do that.

CHAPTER 4

Three Acts

One of the most tried and true methods of plotting is the Three-Act Structure. It has been around since the days of William Shakespeare. Besides books, you will discover that most movies, plays, TV dramas and sit-coms, plus short stories use this well-known method.

The title Three Act structure is a bit misleading because not all the acts are of equal length. Act three is usually the shortest, while Act two is most likely the longest. Act one will vary in its length. Still all three acts have their individual characteristics and uses for the writer.

Let's analyze the three acts and how each is used.

ACT ONE
This is the set up. We use the WHO and the WHAT here as well as the WHEN and WHERE to place the reader in the story.

The WHY will develop more slowly and its full knowledge may not be known until the middle or end of Act Two.

In today's commercial fiction world, the set-up needs to happen quickly. Readers want to know who is involved and what is happening, and they want the information as soon as possible. Gone are the days when you can have a meandering introduction and insert a lot of backstory before you start the plot moving.

While you might be tempted to fill the opening pages with explanations of your foreign world or information about your characters, don't give in. You need to set up your story with action and get the plot moving from the first page. If you want to write a long character sketch, do it as part of the outline, and include it later in the story. But don't start with those two or three pages recalling the past or explaining the character. The same is true of your alien world. Don't spent opening pages explaining how it came into being. Put characters in it and let them show it to the reader.

In the opening pages, you'll want to quickly introduce your characters, give an idea of the setting, start the plot and provide a taste of some of the complications to come. Whether you're dealing with a romance, a romantic suspense or historical story, mystery or paranormal, you must get the plot moving in this first act by providing your *Inciting Incident.*

This is what begins to propel your story forward. From there you are ready to begin causing problems for your characters. No story is told in a simple linear fashion. You will want your characters to succeed in the end, but no one gets there in a straight line. You want them to suffer setbacks and enjoy triumphs all along the way. Your reader wants to see your characters suffer, be challenged and grow as a result.

For example, let's go back to that romance plot we mentioned in the last chapter:

Your heroine has arrived in a new town, hoping to get away from romantic complications and she is all set to begin her new life with her daughter with little interference. But then suddenly there are all sorts of possible complications headed her way. Maybe she finds a body in the house where she is moving, or suddenly she gets word that her family fortune is gone and she must fend for herself. In a romance, it might be meeting the sexy hero next door that begins to complicate her life.

Once we have established the tone of the story, introduced the characters, started things moving, we can focus on ways to keep the plot moving. Does the heroine discover that the hero was owed a great deal of money by her father and now wants to take over her property? Or maybe the body she found was someone who had also claimed her property and now she is accused of killing him.

And what about that intriguing character who lives next door-- why is he intriguing? How will he relate to her? Does he have his own financial problems that will tie him to her so that only by their mutual work together they will survive? Or does she befriend his estranged son and try to bring the two of them together? Perhaps there is an evil landlord who has control over them both and is working to pit them against each other.

As we noted when we discussed motivation, it plays an important role in a story. It is the same here as well. During the first act you will want to set up your character's motivation for why that character is going to pursue a certain course of action.

What is the purpose of your story? That needs to be stated in the first act. Let the reader know where your plot is headed as it gets moving. Provide a direction and show a reason the character might be headed in that direction. Proper motivation can go a long way toward explaining a character's actions. As long as readers know why the character is acting a certain way, they will be ready to follow along for the ride. In our romance, perhaps our heroine feels guilty that she never bothered to communicate with her father so she didn't realize how much trouble he was in financially so now she is determined to hold onto that family land.

You won't necessarily need to keep moving in that same direction through the whole book. In fact, you probably won't want to. To give the first act a wonderful end, you're going to want to turn the action around. You've provided all the necessary details and introduced the characters and a problem. You might even have hinted at what the biggest problems are. Now, to end that first act, turn the action around. Throw everything into turmoil so the reader/viewer will want to continue into the second act.

For instance, at the end of that romance story, perhaps the heroine discovers that the body she found was actually an illegitimate brother who also had claim to the property and now his heirs want a piece of her land. Or perhaps they took her father's money but now they are trying to say she killed him. Maybe she even gets arrested at the end of the first act. Yes, things are really moving along!

ACT TWO

In this act the characters begin to solve the problem, try to find the killer, etc., but run into a series of challenges, both externally (the action scenes) and internally (the conflicts of motivations and the slow change or growth of the character needs to be shown here)

The reader will get to know the protagonist better, either through backstory or by learning about his/her secrets or fears. This is the place to sprinkle in that backstory. Again, you don't want to lump it into a bunch of long narrative sequences, but you can place it carefully through these chapters and scenes to show why a character is behaving in a certain way.

Let's go back to that romance heroine who moved to a new town and ends up with the sexy neighbor next door and the dead half-brother. She is cool to her neighbor, but why? Now we might begin to discover that her old boyfriend was abusive, and maybe he's trying to find her. Or we find out she lost her husband child in a car accident and she doesn't want to love again. And perhaps she questions his motives because he knew all along about her half brother, and didn't tell her up front.

We begin to learn about the character but the action can't stop moving forward either. We need to find realistic reasons for her to interact with that neighbor. Maybe she gets locked out of her house or he agrees to help her in her battle with her half-brother's family. In the movie *Sleeping with the Enemy,* Julia Roberts character is hiding from an abusive husband and is looking for a job. That was all set up in the first act. In the second act, she has traveled across the country and is in a new town. She wants to bake an apple pie and happens to take apples from a neighbor's tree. Enter the hero. But she isn't looking for romance, and while he helps her find a job and she bakes him a pie, she still is trying to keep from getting involved. We know her secret and the reason for her reticence with him, but he certainly doesn't. And then her husband learns she is still alive. Now we know there is more action coming.

These are the sort of twists and turns that need to keep coming through the Second Act of the plot. There needs to be a direction, but feel free to take turns and twist it around. That is what keeps the reader moving through the book.

Remember, Act Two is going to be the longest part of the book. You don't want to make it the most boring as well. This act is where most writers put down the book they're writing. They have hit what is known as the "sagging middle." They started out well and now they suddenly have no place to go. Or if they're writing by the seat of their pants, they find themselves meandering off in all sorts of different directions with no clear cut idea of how to bring the action back to the problem at hand.

There is a purpose for that second act and for making it the longest. This is where you're telling the meat of your story. You'll need to look for ways to keep it moving and to keep the reader interested.

To find ways to combat that sagging middle, look deep into your character's motivation and background. This is why it is so critical to know who the characters are. Test them and let them win some battles or suffer setbacks, but keep the action moving. Don't let the story slow down or you will lose the reader. Make the story or events important to the character. If your scenes further develop the character or make the character grow, the reader will keep going.

In our romance this might be done by developing the relationship between the main characters. She begins to see him in a new light when he helps her fix her damaged roof after a storm, while he appreciates the patience she shows to his son. This would also be the place where they might begin to demonstrate their growing feelings for one another.

As you end your second act, you will again want another twist. In fact this might be where your character suffers the greatest setback. Now you are ready to tackle the final challenge where the character either wins the day or loses everything.

This might be the spot in our romance where after a night of lovemaking, our heroine discovers the hero has secret ties with her half-brother's relatives or once was engaged to his sister so that she begins to question his motives and her own feelings of distrust return, He might think that she is using his son against him. Or perhaps the boy runs away.

ACT THREE

The resolution of the story comes in the final Act. In these scenes the main character comes to grips with his/her internal dilemmas and finds the courage to defeat the enemy. S/he faces the final life or death challenge and succeeds. The final act is where the heroine and/or hero face their inner demons or weakness to combat and overcome whatever challenges might be in front of them. This is where they change and grow in order to achieve their happy conclusion. In the love story we've been outlining, our heroine chooses love and decides to trust the hero, and he grows to trust her when she brings his son home. At this point, they both decide to work together to defeat the half-brother's family and find out where the family fortune really went.

The final scenes in the three act structure may be short, but they are critical. Do you tie up the loose ends for the reader? Is it a happy ending or does it leave the reader wondering? You may do either, but mainly you want to leave the reader wanting to read your next work, no matter what it is.

If you are plotting your book using the three act structure, you will need to figure out your ending so that you know where you are going and how you want things to end. In our romance, the heroine might challenge her half-brother's family and find that one of them killed him because he had discovered they were hiding her money and wanted to tell her the truth. The hero and heroine are united, she has her property back and the hero has made peace with his son because of the new woman in their lives. The ending is happy for all.

USING THE THREE ACT STRUCTURE

The practical benefit of starting to plot your novel using the three act structure is that it helps to put your story in a logical order. You have a firm understanding of your beginning, you get a general idea of what you're doing in the middle and you need to know your ending. Again, as with the 5 W's, even if all you do is to write down the very basics of your story using the three act structure as a guideline, it focuses your story.

If you're using that method, write down as much or as little as you want. It can help you to begin to organize your scenes to see that you are headed in the right direction. If you are confused about how the three act structure works, you can either go through a book of plays to see how they are done or watch television sitcoms or dramas. They are usually arranged in a three-act fashion and you can begin to see how the set is set up, evolves and is resolved in the final act. The last scene is usually an epilogue that shows everything re-solved.

Act one – state the set-up and main character

o   Use the WHO, WHAT and perhaps the WHEN and WHERE

Act two – a few words describing the

o   Backstory and motivation of the main character

o   The action that needs to take place, both external and in-ternal

o   Use the WHY in this act.

Act three – the resolution of the plot and growth of the protag-onist

---

CHAPTER 5

Outline

O utlining is one of the most popular plotting methods. It is simply a plan, a step-by-step, blow-by-blow description of the plot in your book. The secret to outlining is to determine exactly what you want it to be.

An outline could be

o   Scene by scene listing of what you want in your book
o   Random list of the events that need to happen
o   Detailed narrative of the story

You might even take the events from the Three-Act structure and just write them all out so that you have everything put together in one long document. It can be done on your computer, by long hand in a notebook, index cards or even with post-it notes on your office wall.

An outline can be anything from a fistful of handwritten notes to a complex narrative about the plot that is nearly as long as the finished book. Many authors who swear by outlining say they will write up to 100 pages of their outline before they begin to seriously write their novel. The outline may be so complex that they will then use parts of that written outline as sections of the narrative in the book. They might even include carefully crafted scenes in the outline that again can be used in the book.

The outline might contain a detailed picture of the characters as well as their motivations or their backstory. This can help you because the writer then knows exactly where to go to find out what the character looks like or why they are behaving a certain way. By writing an outlined history of that character, the writer gets a complete picture of the person, but the key here is knowing where and what part of that outlined story you want to put into your actual novel. For certain you won't want it in the first chapter of your story. *You* might need to know it, but your reader only needs to know what is essential to make the story plausible.

This is a common mistake that beginning writers make. They will have such a long and detailed outline of their main character that they will forget to put that character into some sort of story or make the action begin to happen. If you are prone to writing a lot about your character, writing a detailed outline of him/her can help get that out of your system. Write it and then set it aside. You can always sprinkle in parts of that description or outline later in your story, once the action has started to move.

The benefit of using an outline are many.

o   It gives you an overall picture of the story

o   It allows you to make changes or place important details along the way

o   It allows you to carefully work on your character's arc...or how your main character is going to change and grow so that by the end of the story s/he has become a better person

o   It lets you see if you are pacing your story properly. Do you give your reader time to catch a breath? Do you have too many boring scenes strung together or conversely, too many action scenes? Notice in any action oriented movie or book, the action is almost always followed by a "quiet" reflective scene.

o   And detailed outline can be used or edited into a synopsis.

In many cases when you get to the final scenes of your book, you may realize something has been left out. With an outline you can easily see those problem areas and go back and introduce the "whatever" so that the ending makes more sense. That way when you actually start to write you know where to put everything or what direction you're heading.

An outline is sort of like a road map you might use at the beginning of a vacation. It has a beginning, the ending spot and then you can select all the little places you want to visit in the middle. Think of a Google or Mapquest map. You can look at the big picture that shows simply the beginning and the line from one spot to another that takes you to the end. If you prefer, you can go in a little closer and see the actual turns on the main thoroughfares, or you can go all the way in and see the actual turns in the streets and where on the street the beginning and ending locations are. Or you can simply use the written directions that list each step along the way.

There is no prescription for the perfect outline. You can decide to do as much or as little as you want. There might be times when all you do is write down what you want to happen. Her brother is killed. How is he killed? An accident? A murder? An accident made to look like a murder? Where did the weapon come from?

Or perhaps you want to go into great detail about what the murder scene looked like so that you know what clues will trip up the killer later in the story. Again, having these written down someplace can help you as you write your story to get it to flow properly.

Outlining can be very beneficial when plotting a mystery or a thriller. It allows the author to make certain clues are placed and shows places where the plot might need to be turned in another direction. Thrillers and mysteries are often very tightly plotted so that the story is constantly on the move and headed in a particular direction.

An outline can also be very helpful when trying to figure out relationships, say in a romance. Times have changed from the old days when the story can get off to a slow start and the hero and heroine don't get together for a while. Current readers want the main characters in a romance to meet quickly so the writer needs to figure out how to make that happen without making the beginning seem false or contrived. When should the first kiss happen? What about sex scenes? This is also complicated by the need for motivation. Strong feelings are not going to grow out of mere proximity or even sexual appeal. The characters need to drive the romance and that means a plot that uses or demonstrates feelings and emotions to go along with the physical actions.

An outline can also be invaluable when dealing with subplots. Weaving in a sub-plot with minor characters may require a detailed outline to keep the action separate and yet tied to the main plot.

Finally, one of the big benefits of writing out an outline is that the writer can pull out parts of it or use it when writing a synopsis to send to agents and editors.

CHAPTER *6*

Plot Points

lot points are very similar to an outline, and can even be used
to build an eventual outline. These are usually quick sentences that show the protagonist in action or that motivate
him/her to do something. These are more like those Mapquest or
Google map directions that list each frame of action.

PLOT POINTS are happenings that form the framework of the
book. They can be e external/action oriented and cause great conflict
and great trouble for the protagonist or they can be moments of
reflection that prompt action

A few plot points might be:

o   the inciting incident

o   the first problem/crisis/dilemma that the character must
face a severe crisis

o   a setback for your character

o   an emotional discovery

o   a critical meeting between two characters

o   an important event that sends the plot in a new direction

o   a fight scene where the main character wins/loses/is hurt

o   an emotional confrontation

o   a love scene

o   the character's change

o   the climax

o   the resolution

If we expand on several of these important plot points they might become:

The inciting incident
it is the reason the main character decides to go on the quest/solve the problem or find the killer

The first problem/crisis/dilemma that the character must face
here the turning point is that the character must overcome/cope with the problem...sometimes s/he fails, sometimes s/he gets help

A severe crisis

now the character is finally getting to know the problem; however s/he must now face the possibility that what they are doing may be the wrong path and they need to change directions

The character's change

the epiphany that changes the character's view of the situation.

The plot points can also be used to build a list of scenes. Let's look back at that romance we used in the three-act structure::

o   Gina moves to a new town

o   She meets Clint who lives next door with his quiet, rebellious son

o   She discovers Clint has placed a lien on her property because her father owed him money

o   Together they discover a dead body in the basement

We won't go into all the details, but you can see from this list the various written out points we were giving as we developed the earlier story. The great thing about plot points is that you can always move them around if you find out the plot is not working.

Let's deconstruct a couple of popular movies as a way of showing how to use plot points to begin plotting your story.

In *Star Wars* some of the plot points are:

o   Luke and his uncle buy the droids

o   R-2 D-2 runs off and Luke goes to find it

o   He is saved by Obi Wan when he is attacked

o   Luke finds his aunt and uncle have been killed

o   He and Obi Wan hire Han Solo to take them to Alderan

o   Along the way, Obi Wan teaches Luke about the Force

o   They find Alderan destroyed

o   The Millenium Falcon is captured by the Empire

o   Luke and Han rescue the Princess from her cell

o   Obi Wan must disable the force field so they can escape

o   Obi Wan meets Darth Vader and is killed

o   Obi Wan is killed

o   Luke, Han and the Princess escape the Death Star

o   They rejoin the rebels who plan to destroy it

o   Han leaves to pay Jabba

o   Luke joins the mission to destroy the Death Star

o   Han returns and helps Luke

o   Luke uses the Force to destroy the Death Star

In *The Wizard of Oz*, some of the plot points are:

o   Dorothy laments her life and wishes for a better place

o   She runs away from home when her dog is taken

o   A cyclone lands Dorothy in Oz

o   She finds the red slippers on her feet

o   The Wicked Witch threatens her

o   She sets off for Oz so he can help her get home

o   Dorothy meets the Scarecrow

o   They stop to gather apples

o   They find the Tin Man

o   They are attacked by the Wicked Witch

o   They meet the Cowardly Lion

o   They get to the Emerald City

o   They meet the Wizard who sends them on a quest to get the broom

o   Dorothy is is captured by the winged monkeys

o   She kills the witch

o   The Wizard turns out to be a fraud

o   She is sent home by her thoughts

Like in outlining, the plot points can be as simple or complex as the writer chooses. They might be an entire scene or they might be part of a scene and the scene is made up of two or more plot points.

For instance:

Scene One
Jane arrives home, tired and all she wants is a nice bath.
She opens her bathroom door and finds a dead body
It's a total stranger.

The writer can either list all the plot points in numerical order or simply in order as a timeline. The plot points again can be as detailed or as sparse as the writer chooses. The writer can then go back later and look over the plot points and perhaps group them together to see what might be in a scene or what even list the plot points according to chapter.

If writing a mystery, the writer might want to go back through and decide which elements are going to be included as actual scenes, and which might have happened that the hero or heroine doesn't find out about until later.

For instance, take those three points just described where Jane comes home and finds the body. Separate plot points might describe or list what actually happened and then Jane will unravel the mystery as the story unfolds. As the writer, you would need to know who that person was and how it happened. By putting that part into plot points you'll be able to build your story.

Plot points can also work very well with the narrative outline. Again using the three points listed, the writer might then decide to explain in detail in their written outline who the body is or even write down the details of what Jane sees in the bathroom for later use.

The benefit of using plot points is that the writer can quickly write down all the events or action that need to happen in the book and then go back later and either fill in the details or explain why something happened.

Again, this device can help the writer see where there might be plot holes. This method can also help the writer look for places where the pacing might need to be picked up or to slow down. Some writers will place A next to action scenes or put the action scenes in one color and the reflective scenes in another color.

If there are too many action spots, the writer might choose to give the hero or heroine (as well as the reader) a breather.

When we mentioned the plot being the skeleton of a story, plot points might be considered the actual bones, the bits and pieces that are all strung together to make a living, walking person.

Let's see how an outline with its plot points might have been developed for *Romancing the Stone*. In this case we are going to include some plot points that won't be used as a scene in the story itself, but that are necessary for the story to start.

o   Sister's husband mails Joan the "map" (we don't see this happen)

o   Sister is kidnapped (this happens as the story starts and is needed to give Joan, the main protagonist, the motivation to save her)

o   Joan is writing a book about a feisty heroine and rugged action hero

o   Joan finishes her book and celebrates with her cat.

o   Map arrives in the mail

o   Joan visits her publisher who wants her to look for a "real" man.

o   Joan's apartment is vandalized

o   Joan gets a frantic call from her sister that she needs to take the map to her.

o   Joan goes to Colombia

o   Joan takes the wrong bus

o   The bus breaks down

o   Joan is rescued by Jack Colton

etc., etc......

These are all very quick sentences that show how the story starts to move. An example of a narrative outline might be very similar but contain more detail.

Joan Wilder is a romance novelist who writes adventurous tales about a feisty heroine and a rugged hero. She is a bestselling novelist but she lives alone in New York with her cat. She has just finished her latest book and is taking it to her publisher when she gets mail from her dead brother in law. Her publisher thinks she should get involved with a man of her own rather than living through her characters.

Get the picture? One is telling the action, while the other method of plotting is giving a more detailed description of the character and the plot itself. Either will work just as those map instructions should take you to your destination.

Finally, just remember that because you have an outline or have made all your plot points, you don't need to be a slave to them. Give yourself the creative freedom to wander off in a new direction. If, as you're writing your story, you find a certain plot point doesn't work, then go a different way. By having the plot points already lined up or your outline already completed, you can see where you need to make changes to get the story to work before you ever start to write your novel.

CHAPTER 7

Storyboards

A storyboard is a visual picture, map of sorts, of your story and one of the best "tools" you can develop and use. It allows you to fine-tune your plot because it is composed of moveable ideas.

The best way to set up a storyboard is to buy a trifold display board at your local office or craft store. They are cheap. Then rule off squares using the next page as an example.

However, these are many other ways to set up a story board.

o   Use any door, whether it be to the bathroom or a back door in the kitchen or the door in your bedroom

o   Use any wall in any room. Ideally one where you write would be perfect, but once again any empty wall works well, and sticky notes don't leave marks

o   A dining room table can work, although it's a bit harder to see the overall picture on a flat surface.

o   A cardboard table that you lean again a chair also works well

Next, use sticky notes to write on. These work well, as you can move them around as the story develops and comes together. Use different colors for different characters and events--blue for the hero, pink for the heroine and perhaps purple for the villain. Green is great for the action plot points while yellow works for the emotional reactions.

Some writers use index cards instead of sticky notes and either tack or scotch tape them to the board or wall. You can use the 3 x 5 index cards or if you need them larger, try the 5 x 7 cards. They can easily be taken down and shuffled or lined up beside your computer for easy use once you have them in the proper order.

The biggest advantage of the storyboard is that your plot is all laid out in front of you and you can follow it along as you write. It also allows you to "correct" or fix problems before you start writing your story

For instance, the heroine needs to know how to shoot a gun to kill the bad guy in the next to last scene. Maybe she already knows how to shoot. Let's say she was a sharp-shooter in college, or her father had taught her how when she was growing up, or maybe she was robbed or attacked and our hero took time to teach her how to shoot.

But where do you put this knowledge? You can't simply "tell" the reader she puts the bullet between the bad guy's eyes in the last scene. No. The reader has to know prior to that last scene that she knows how to shoot.

So go back to the storyboard and add another sticky note where you tell the reader she knows how to shoot. Perhaps you have a scene where she goes to a shooting range on her day off work.

The storyboard is a great help in de-tangling your plot also. It helps to keep track as you move along. Even if you don't plot too much, you might try making a storyboard as you write the story. This is a great way to see where you might need to go back and drop in red herrings, extra villains or new friends.

Finally, one the greatest advantages of the storyboard is to track the growth of the protagonist. By using one color for his/her internal and emotional change, you can see how it progresses during the course of the story.

We don't want the character's growth to happen all at once. It should come in small spurts along the way. Putting this on a sticky note in one color will help the writer keep track of it more easily.

An example of a storyboard:

Example of a story board

Inciting Incident - the start of the action and setting up the world with time and setting	Introduce main character	Decision by the main character to move forward and solve the problem, complication or dilemma	Some type of a problem either happens or occurs *(this can be either external or internal)*
Reaction of the main character and how s/he tried to solve this problem	A bit of back story Supporting characters introduced	Start of a relationship	Another problem occurs
Reaction of the main character as s/he gets deeper in the situation	More back story	Relationship between the main characters becomes serious	More problems and these tend to be more serious
Still no great solutions arise	Character starts to take control of the situation	Secret(s) exposed/ explained	No turning back
Epiphany Definitive change/ growth/maturing of protagonist	Black Moment	Climax wherein secrets or fears are finally put to rest and bad guys are defeated or killed	Conclusion with final resolution of all loose ends

Here is an example using plot points:

Here is an example of a romance using plot points

• Set up world • Introduce main character/characters • Inciting Incident	• Introduce awareness or conflict between main characters • Conflict needs to be strong and powerful	• Introduce other characters or problems • Include attraction	• First Major Plot Point which will turn into a major Turning Point (T.P.) *(this can be either external or internal)*
• Reaction of the main character to T.P. • Characters warm up to each other but each one feels the other one doesn't like them	• Much more attraction is needed and this is starting to offset the conflict	• Relationship is explored, maybe first kiss or the glow from thinking at least one of them is in love	• Second T.P. • Perhaps first sex scene which they soon decide was a mistake
• Reactions	• Backstory • Reasons why they shouldn't fall in love	• Other characters get involved, some on her side, some on his side • Or an old love comes back into the picture	• Third T.P. • One of them goes off with old love to simply resolve some issues, but other character "reads" it wrong and gets upset
• Reaction of the main character to T. P. • Decision that needs to be made	• Character changes character beginning to become evident • Fears or flaws are now in the open. They decide they are too different.	• Secret(s) exposed • Events that could lead with character to change their beliefs or core problems	• Final T.P. • Something happens that either pulls them apart or forces them together in order to solve the outside problem
• Epiphany • Definitive change/ growth/maturing of both characters • Lessons are learned	• Black Moment • Emotional despair • One or both realize all is lost	• Climax • Secrets or fears are finally explained and put to rest	• Conclusion with final resolution of all loose ends • Relationship is back on track and all ends well

Here is a storyboard for the movie, *Romancing the Stone:*

Here is a storyboard for the movie, *Romancing the Stone*

• We learn that Joan writes romances, but that she has never had one of her own	• Joan must go to Columbia and return a map to save her sister	• She arrives, but gets on the wrong bus and we learn that she is being followed	• Bus breaks down and bad guy tries to steal her map
• Joan is saved by Jack who demands money to take her to Cartegena • Colonel Zolo arrives on the scene	• They escape through the jungle and Jack hacks off her shoes and tosses her suitcase away • Colonel Zolo and his army chase them	• They struggle to get through the jungle with Colonel Zolo's men right behind them • They come to an impassable ravine	• Joan takes a chance and flies across the ravine on a vine • Jack follows her and they escape the bad guys
• Joan tells Jack about her sister's dilemma and the map • He tells her his dream of buying a sailboat • He studies the map	• They get to a village where Jack learns about her popularity as a writer • He tries to make a copy of the map	• They must escape the Colonel and his men again • They discover they are near the treasure	• They arrive at another village where there is a festival going on and they decide to go after the treasure themselves after making love
• The bad guys show up and a chase follows	• They follow the clues on the map and find a worthless trinket	• They find the jewel after Joan uses a plot idea from one of her novels	• They are chased, jump into the river and are separated • Joan goes to Cartegena but Jack doesn't show up
• She takes the map to the bad guys and gets her sister back, but Zolo shows up with a captured Jack • Crocodile swallows the jewel	• Black Moment - the bad guys are ready to kill them • Joan saves her sister, while Jack decides to go after the crocodile and the jewel	• Joan goes home and finishes her book • Jack disappeared after going after the crocodile	• Jack comes to get Joan in his new sailboat wearing crocodile boots

Here is a storyboard for the movie *Star Wars, A New Hope:*

Here is a storyboard for the movie *Star Wars, A New Hope*

• Princess sends a message with the two droids before she is captured • Luke and uncle buy the droids	• Luke tells his uncle he wants to be a pilot and leave the farm • Luke finds the Princess' message before one of the droids runs off	• Luke goes to find the droid and is attacked • He is saved by Obi Wan and they hear Princess Leia's plea	• Luke's aunt and uncle are killed
• Luke decides to go with Obi Wan and they meet with Han Solo • They are pursued as they leave the planet	• As they travel Luke finds out about the *"force"* and tries to learn how to use it • Han reveals himself as a callous smuggler wanting only money	• They reach Alderan only to find it has been destroyed • They are captured by the Death Star	• R2-D2 tells them the Princess is here and they go to rescue her but • They end up in the garbage disposal
• The droids try to get them out	• Obi Wan goes to disable the Force Field so they can escape	• Obi Wan meets his old friend/enemy Darth Vader	• Obi Wan is killed by Darth Vader
• Luke, Hand and Leia escape and go to the rebel base	• They take the plans for the Death Star to the rebels who plan to attack it	• Han, who was only in the battle for the money, leaves	• Luke and the rebels go to destroy the Death Star
• In the air fight, Darth Vader is after Luke		• Luke must put his trust in the *"force"* as he tries to destroy the Death Star	• Death Star is destroyed and Han and Luke are heroes

CHAPTER 8

Backward Plotting

Plotting from the end to the beginning might seem impossible, especially since many writers don't have any idea how their story is going to end. They simply begin with a general idea and may start writing, hoping to figure out the end along the way.

However, knowing the ending of your story before you finish your book can be very helpful by making the writer decide what has to happen in the book in order for this ending to ring true to the reader. It can greatly speed up the editing process because you're able to make certain that necessary elements are already written into the story.

Depending on the genre, what conclusion is necessary for the tale to have a satisfactory ending? To do this, start by asking yourself: What is the object of the story?

The objective of a plot is to have a clear statement of where you want the story to end.

In a **romance,** the ending most likely will be the typical happy ending. The hero and heroine will, after overcoming a series of obstacles and emotionally maturing, declare their love for each other and decide to live happily ever after.

In a **thriller** or **mystery** novel, the ending will be when the killer is killed, caught or brought to justice or the virus/bomb threat is neutralized. If the villain escapes (which is often done for a series) the immediate threat must be handled or gone.

In a **sci-fi, fantasy,** or **paranormal** story, any ending is possible from winning the war, finding a brave new world, to stopping the robots from taking over the planet or de-activating the magic spell.

In some cases the writer can get away with leaving little loose ends, but not usually. For instance, in *Silence of the Lambs,* Thomas Harris leaves Hannibal Lector on the loose. However, he makes it clear that Hannibal is not going to go after Claire, but it certainly sets the stage for a sequel. This sort of ending can often be used when writing a book that is one of a series.

Knowing the ending allows the author to fill in all the appropriate and necessary elements to make these endings work. To build a backward plot, you still need to start with knowing the basics about your characters, remember the five W's, and a bit about what genre and theme you are going to use. If you start at the end you will know how your characters change or grow to meet the final challenge. From here you can build backward until you decide where you want your characters (and the story) to start.

Do you want your heroine to finally get a backbone and stand up to her overbearing mother/step-father/guardian? What does that mean she was like at the beginning of the book? What are the steps you are going to need to take get her from that first stage to your ending?

Knowing what conclusion you want to reach allows you to:

o   list the things that have to happen/be included to reach this conclusion

o   add "red herrings" and false leads and characters to keep the plot moving

o   put in what is needed in the set-up for the conclusion to work

(For example, if the heroine shoots the villain during the final climax, somewhere along the way, the reader will need to know how she got the gun, if she can shoot it and where it is kept...as the gun can't suddenly appear nor can she be a "crack shot" unless some ground work/backstory has been woven in.)

Perhaps one of the best things about plotting backward or beginning with the end is that it allows you to take lots of time with thinking things through and putting extra effort into those final scenes. Finishing a novel can be tough work and too often a writer will just end the book without giving it the full attention it needs. The writer is in such a rush to finish the story that important details might be ignored or forgotten. Writing from the back forward helps to correct this problem.

While the first pages of a book might make a reader want to keep reading THIS book, a great ending can make the reader want to buy your NEXT book.

Plotting backward is like opening a map. Your destination is place X, a number of miles from where you live. So before you pack the car, you spread the map out on the kitchen table, take out a red marker and carefully mark out the route.

So it is with a backward plot. Only now, you start at your destination and use that marker to find your way home.

Even if you don't plot using this method, you still might consider your ending or determine what it will be as you start to plot using one of the other methods even before you fill in the middle portion. As we noted, knowing what the conclusion will be can help you make certain you don't leave out critical scenes that are necessary to your plot. Also, if you know how your character grows and changes, you can then plot scenes to make that happen earlier in your book.

CHAPTER 9

No Plotting

Having looked at most of the ways writers plot, let's look at one that has no form at all—simply writing off the top of your head or by the seat of your pants.

Sometimes the whole process of outlining is too difficult and the writer simply wants to sit down and start to write. In fact, as we've noted, some writers say that once they've put their plot down in an outline form, they feel like the book is finished and they have a hard time going back to actually write it.

Writing without an outline is the simple and most basic form of writing. The writer has an idea or perhaps a character and sits down at the keyboard and begins typing up the story. Where will it go? What will happen next? The writer lets whatever fancy hits him/her at the time make that decision.

Some writers feel that too much plotting takes away their freedom to simply create. Never quite knowing where the character will lead the writer, is what makes writing enjoyable for them. For many writers s the thrill of an unexpected scene or development in the story line is what makes them want to keep writing.

Call it stream of consciousness, free form or just putting down random thoughts, no plotting is great for short exercises or getting down random scenes, and many writers have been successful using this form of plotting or "no plotting."

However it can be dangerous for the beginner because there is the tendency to get lost, bogged down or totally confused about what has happened and what they want to happen. When writing free form like this, the writer may have to go back and go through the book and start putting together the events into a cohesive string.

Writing a story without a plan is like building a house. If you begin with no diagram or blueprint, you can end up with all these crazy corners and angles or hallways going nowhere. There might be useless walls or they're not going to meet exactly with the ceiling. You might find yourself with no bathroom or no way to get to it even if it's included.

This is not to imply that the no-plotting method can't work. On the plus side, it is often fun to write this way. Most writers who have been around for a while may be able to write without an outline once they get a feel for their characters or where they want to go. Some people will use a variation of a loose outline or the plot points and then simply begin to write.

Knowing there is always the option of letting the outline go or forgetting about the story board can sometimes free an author to be more creative. On the other hand, what if you suddenly reach a point and your imagination goes blank. Suddenly you don't know what you want to do next and nothing you've written so far is work-ing. That is when lots of people just shove the book under the bed.

On the other hand if you have a general idea of where you want to go, or even if you generally know where the character has to go, and what has to happen to this character, simply sitting down to write the story can take the form of writing that detailed outline. You simply add the dialogue along the way. If you know the ending, you have a point to aim for and that can make writing without a plot formula work also. You know where you want to eventually end up so you can start writing and think about how you want to get there as you go along.

You can also use other methods in conjunction with the No Plot-ting method. For instance, after each day or week of writing, you might go back and make up a list of the plot points or a chap-ter/scene breakdown. That way if you do find yourself at a standstill you can go back and look at places where you might have gone wrong and fix them.

The benefit about writing without a plot is that when you're done with the plot, the book is done as well.

These are **seven various plotting methods** but they are by no means the only ways to plot a story. All you have to do is Google "plotting methods" and you will come up with many more systems.

These range from templates to pyramids and snowflakes, to using a fairy tale as a starting point as well as first doing a synopsis to the best ways to use colored index cards.

We've said it before, but it bears repeating -- what works for one writer may or may not work for another scribe. You should try the methods that appeal to you or even try them all until you find one that fits both your personality and the way you write and think. Emotional writing hats also play an important part in determining which method or system you finally decide to use.

But no matter which method you decide to use, there are certain things you keep in mind. Here are twelve questions you need to "think about" as you develop your plot. Think about each of these carefully. You might even consider writing each one on an index card and over the next few weeks craft answers to them. It's interesting to note that you may develop several different answers to each question. As your plot develops in your mind, think about these questions as they also concern the other characters in your story.

We often think that only the hero and the heroine need to be emotionally developed with flaws and problems. But don't forget the villain—that character also needs these questions answered if you really want a memorable antagonist.

1 - What goal/dream/prize does your character want? This is usually something out of his/her reach but nevertheless is something they truly desire. This may also change from the beginning of the story.

2 - What problem/dilemma/mystery/puzzle happens that completely changes your character's world? Turns his/her very life upside-down. (The Inciting Incident)

3 - What does your character have to do, either physically or emotionally, to try to solve the problem, find the treasure, capture the killer or save the "damsel in distress?"

4 - What friend/lover/enemy will help the most at finding the solution/answer to the problem?

5 - Are the villain's goal(s) in direct opposition to your character's wants and needs?

6 - What secret or flaw haunts your character? This should be a really big secret or a flaw he/she can overcome.

7 - What terrible, "out of character" act will your character do to keep his/her secret a secret whether it is a big or small secret?

8 - What internal emotion/action is released when your character's secret or flaw is revealed?

9 - Name several conflicts that will discourage your character from continuing on his/her journey? Start with small ones and work up to the bigger ones.

10 - What final complication/conflict/event makes the quest seem hopeless?

11 - What lesson does your character have to learn? How is s/he going to learn this lesson? And how will this change the character? This can also be the flaw that needs to be corrected.

12 - What final decision does your character have to make to "save the day?" Of course it should be a difficult decision and one that s/he doesn't necessarily like but one that is in keeping with the change in his/her personality.

If you go through the various methods suggestions in this booklet and try them out, you should have a better understanding of plotting and how to get started on your book. If these don't work for you, then you might investigate some of the other methods out there, and as we mentioned, there are a good many of them. You might also combine methods to come up with a new idea all your own. It's all up to you. We hope we've provided you with enough of the basics so that no matter which method you decide will work for you, in the end you discover an easy, basic, quick method to plot your next book.

Good luck in your plotting adventure.

Examples

Following are a few of the more common plots. We are combining books and movies here to give you a more complete idea of what to look for in a plot.

Adventure

The adventure plot is about a journey the protagonist takes, usually to find his fortune or to recover something. It involves the action that is connected with the journey. The journey must be larger, more exciting, and more important than the character and feature a colorful location that rings authentic.

Eragon
The Wind in the Willows

Betrayal

In the betrayal plot a trust is broken or perhaps badly smashed/destroyed. One of the characters makes the difficult decision, usually for a very personal and compelling reason, to betray the other person. This often happens in a love triangle story. Many spy or political traitor tales are based on some sort of betrayal.

Clear and Present Danger
The Social Network

Coming of Age

This plot is about outside events and/or emotional problems that force the protagonist to evolve, grow up, and become more responsible. Innocent, naive, or perhaps in an uncompromising mind-set, the protagonist is propelled, either by the story action or by an older and wiser mentor, to alter his or her thinking to come of age and mature.

The Lion King
To Kill a Mockingbird

Conversion

This plot centers on someone or something that is either altered or changed, or is a character who reinvents him or herself. The story revolves around the process of conversion so that at the end of the story, the character is transformed into a new and different person or has learned to emotionally live with the change.

A Christmas Carol
The Princess Diaries

Disaster

A disaster plot takes many forms from man-made problems, such as a nuclear accident or unleashed viruses, to natural problems that are planet-related or caused by failed technology. One hero or team has to have the scientific or special knowledge that will allow them to save the day, the planet, or somehow avoid the catastrophe.

Jurassic Park
Outbreak

Discovery

The discovery plot is about a protagonist's search to understand who he is and why he is here. It is more about the character and less about the journey. The character is forced to use his skills and faculties to overcome extremely unusual situations where he may also need to overcome his fears and trust in his own abilities.

Philadelphia
Red Badge of Courage

Escape

In an escape plot the victim must be able to free her/himself without outside help. The protagonist is usually confined against his will and wants or needs to somehow escape. The plot concentrates on the mechanics of the capture, the imprisonment (where and for how long) and the final method or process of escape.

Shawshank Redemption
Escape from Alcatraz

Quest

The quest plot is a journey in which the protagonist is searching for a person, place or a physical object. It may also be a quest for an intangible such as his or her soul. This journey, whether done out of necessity or by a great desire, is long, involves many others along the way and many times includes a close friend.

The Wizard of Oz
Lord of the Rings

Pursuit

The pursuit plot is about one person or one thing, such as a car or an alien, chasing someone or something for a definite reason. The game of hide and seek is played, and the protagonist may be either the hunter trying to catch the villain or the victim trying to elude the bad guys. Usually this is a fast-paced action story full of chases.

The Fugitive
Les Miserables

Puzzle

In the puzzle plot the mystery is determined and a search for clues will lead the protagonist to find the missing piece or catch the killer. However, the clues should be well-hidden and ambiguous so that only by the keen insight and deductive reasoning of the protagonist can the answer be found, the solution finally achieved, or the killer exposed.

Matrix
Sherlock Holmes

Relationships

The relationship plot involves two protagonists and the difficulty they face in being together, whether it involves overcoming obstacles created by the social mores and taboos of the times they live in or their own personal, emotional obstacles. This might include such problems as physical and/or emotional limitations, being the same gender, differences in age, skin color, religious beliefs, or social status. Emotional issues might include mistrust, fear of love, or something in their past.

The Notebook
Brokeback Mountain

Rescue

The rescue plot is all action and involves the protagonist searching and trying to save someone or something from danger. The threat can be physical, emotional or spiritual. The main character, who finally succeeds in rescuing the person or thing, may also in some way rescue himself from his own personal threat.

The Poseidon Adventure
The Princess Bride

Revenge

The revenge plot involves a protagonist retaliating against a wrong or a perceived wrong. It might be as simple as a confrontation or it can involve an elaborate plan. Success usually depends on the failings of the evildoer as well as the cleverness of the protagonist. It may also be the villain who is planning the revenge.

The Man in Iron Mask
The Count of Monte Cristo

Rivalry

The rivalry plot is when two characters of equal strength and intelligence share or covet the same object, person, power, or wealth and they compete for this goal until it takes over their lives. It might be God versus Satan in a struggle for a person's soul, two politicians vying for the same office, or two competing teams trying to win a game.

Ben-Hur

The Hunger Games

Sacrifice

In a sacrifice plot the characters give service, either mental or physical, to a higher authority, a cause, or an ideal. Usually this story has religious undertones and is filled with moral decisions. Love and honor are also sacrifice themes and quite often these stories do not have a happy ending but try to teach the reader a moral lesson.

The Chronicles of Narnia

Schindler's List

Underdog

An underdog plot features a protagonist who is at a great disadvantage and is faced with overwhelming odds. The plot focuses on the evolution of the protagonist seeking a goal. Usually in this plot, the character is not the great genius or even superman, he or she is an ordinary person fighting/striving simply to win the prize.

Rocky

Odd Thomas

Excerpts

B EFORE YOU GO...

Thank you for reading SEVEN WAYS TO PLOT. We hope you enjoyed it and are ready to start your own writing project!

In the **Dottie's** *Let's Write a Story* series the following books are soon to out:

Creating Memorable Characters

The Plotting Wheel

Creating Great Villains

✎ ✎ ✎ ✎ ✎ ✎

EXCERPT from the next booklet, *CREATING MEMORABLE CHARACTERS*

Whoever is telling the story, the writer needs to remember to put the POV into the hands of the character who has the most to gain or lose in each scene. It makes each scene stronger and more vivid in the mind of the reader if only one POV is used in the entire scene.

The differences between the sexes and their POV

-Women see the world through an array of vivid emotions

Huge crocodile tears rolled down her cheeks as she learned of her grandfather's death knowing that she had been too busy, too involved with her own life, to visit him over the past few months.

-Men view the world through their actions

Upon hearing of his grandfather's death, he began making the funeral arrangements.

- Women make suggestions

She smiled shyly as she glanced at her lover and asked, "Why don't we have lunch now?"

- Men make statements

"Let's go to lunch," he said starting to leave the room.

- Women tend to be more emotional in their statements.

"I hope Helen is in a good mood. I get so frustrated when she starts on one of her rants."

- Men tend to be more factual and logical in their statements

"Have you thought about what will happen if you go to Helen's?"

Who do you determine which character's POV is best to use?

o   Choose the character who has the most to lose in the scene, not the character

who has the most to gain.

o   If you are having trouble deciding, try writing the scene in first person

- *first in one character's POV*

- *then do the same scene, still in first person, in the other character's POV*

o   Or if you still can't decide,
       try the scene in the POV of the character who is simply observing
       an emotional crisis involving the other character

End of Excerpt

ABOUT THE AUTHORS

Sue Viders

Sue has a BFA in education and fine arts and is the author of over 25 books - all nonfiction. She has also written extensively for a variety of magazines and newspapers. A national columnist for many years on art marketing in *The Artist's Magazine*, Sue has spoken to various groups and organizations both nationally and internationally on marketing and writing for over thirty-five years. She continues to lecture and teach writing, both onsite at colleges and universities as well as at national conferences. She regularly teaches online through numerous writing groups and organizations throughout the world.

Her books for writers include:
o   *The Complete Writer's Guide to HEROES and HERO-INES, Sixteen Master Archetypes*

o   *The Whole Writer's Building Blocks for Nonfiction* series (coming out in 2016)
o   *Deal a Story,* a card game for writers based on the Heroes and Heroines Archetype book.

Meg and the Mysterious Voices, is the first in a series of light-hearted cozy mysteries revolving around Meg Jamison, a middle-aged artist with an interesting hearing aid, a pair of silver earrings that allows Meg to not only hear better but to hear a person's inner thoughts.

For more information on the Meg Jamison series go to http://dbhumel.com and receive a FREE prequel about Meg when you sign up for her newsletter.

✎ ✎ ✎ ✎ ✎ ✎

Becky Martinez

Becky Martinez, who writes as Rebecca Grace, is a former broadcast journalist who has worked in TV newsrooms around the west. After 30 years she left the newsroom for five years in public relations before turning to the world of fiction writing full time. She is published in mystery, romance, and romantic suspense. She also teaches writing classes online and has presented workshops at a number of writing conferences, including the RWA National Conference, RomCon, Colorado Gold, the Emerald Cities Writers Conference and she has presented panels at

Left Coast Crime and the Pikes Peak Writers Conference.

Her latest book, *Blues at 11*, is a humorous mystery, set in the world of a Los Angeles television journalist. It was published by The Wild Rose Press in January 2015. *What happens when a well-known TV anchorwoman finds herself suspected of murder?*

Her previous book, *Dead Man's Rules,* was also published by The Wild Rose Press and is set in a small fictional New Mexico town. *When a TV tabloid reporter goes searching for answers to an old mystery she uncovers long held secrets that just might rip a small town apart.*
Becky has also had several short stories and novellas published. Her short story, "Trouble in the Rockies" was part of the anthology, The *Trouble with Romance,* which was a New Mexico Book Award finalist. Her latest short story, "One More Romance," is part of an anthology, *Sealed with Love,* which was published in May 2015 by the Heart of Denver Romance Writers.

She is currently working on the second book in the *Blues* series and a follow up to *Dead Man's Rules.*

She has a weekly blog, My Writing Corner, http://www.rebecca-grace.blogspot.com and her latest classes and works are listed on her website at http://www.rebeccagrace.com

FREE WORKSHEETS

We have developed a series of worksheets to go with each of the seven plotting methods in this book. They are FREE for you to use. All you have to do is request them. These worksheets come in an email Word file and are perfect for any computer, or you can print them out if you prefer to handwrite your ideas.

To get your set of worksheets, please send us an email at letswriteastory05@gmail.com and we will email them to you.

Follow us on our monthly blog, http://www.letswriteastorywDottie.blogspot.com

Also you can sign up for our quarterly newsletter and you will be entered in a drawing for a chance to win a copy of a future "Let's Write a Story" booklet.

And finally, our writing classes will be starting soon. Watch for the announcement in our newsletter.

🖋 🖋 🖋 🖋 🖋 🖋

NONFICTION BOOKS and GAMES for Writers

BOOKS

The Complete Writer's Guide to Heroes and Heroines, Sixteen Master Archetypes

Available both in print and digital format
Available on Amazon
http://goo.gl/ElyB4x

By following the guidelines presented in this comprehensive reference work, writers can create extraordinarily memorable characters. Throughout the book, there are examples of well known heroes and heroines from TV and film. The book's guidelines provide insight into how archetypes are formed and how they interact with other archetypes.

CARD GAME

Deal a Story -- A Brainstorming Card Game

Robert D. Reed Publishers
www.dealastory.com

The game is based on the Hero and Heroine archetypes and

consists of 101cards. There are six categories: heroes, heroines, villains, genre, plots, and flaws, each containing 16 cards. When mixed and matched, the writer has the beginnings of a story. Great for learning how to think out-of-the-box and for writing groups. I'm especially proud of this card game as it gives writers a neat way to "think" out-of-the-old box. Available at http://www.rdrpublishers.com

FICTION BOOKS

Sue Viders
   The Meg Jamison Mysteries – under the name of D.B. Humel
   All will be available on Amazon both in print and as ebooks
   Prequel - FREE - Meg and the Blue Fingers
   Book 1 - Meg and the MysteriousVoices
   Book 2 - Meg and the Misguided Arsonist
   Book 3 - Meg and the Missing Locket

Becky Martinez
   All are available at www.bn.com, www.amazon.com or
   www.thewildrosepress.com
   Blues at 11 – The Wild Rose Press – January 2015
   Dead Man's Rules – The Wild Rose Press – May 2014
   Shadows from the Past – The Wild Rose Press – October 2013

The Problem – The Wild Rose Press – June 2011
Deadly Messages – The Wild Rose Press – 2010
Home Fires Burning – Wings ePress – 2010
One More Romance -- Heart of Denver Romance Writers
Anthology

www.ingramcontent.com/pod-product-compliance
Lightning Source LLC
Chambersburg PA
CBHW021140020426

42331CB00005B/851